In The Beginning

GOOD BOOK PRESS · LOS ANGELES, CALIFORNIA

ISBN: 0-89287-111-3

First Printing August 1976
Second Printing October, 1977

M.L.V. = Modern Language Version
K.J.V. = King James Version

Photography: David Muench
Design: Bonnie Muench
Text: Rev. Robert Langbauer, M. Div.
Graphics: James O. Sullivan

Good Book Press · 222 North Virgil Avenue · Los Angeles, California 90004

In the beginning . . .

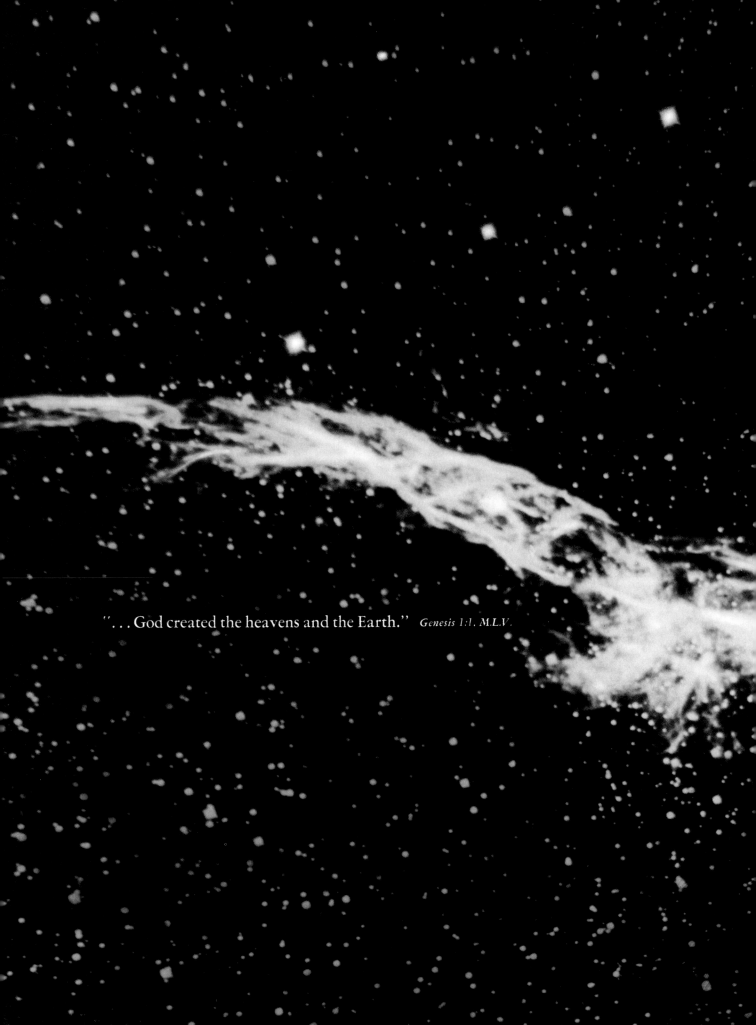

"...God created the heavens and the Earth." *Genesis 1:1. M.L.V.*

"and darkness lay upon the face of the deep . . .

. . . and the spirit of God moved upon the face of the waters.'' *Genesis 1:2, K.J.V.*

"God said let there be light, and there was light.
God saw the light was good
. . . and the light God called Day."

Genesis 1:3-5, M.L.V.

Bless the Lord, O my soul! O Lord my God, thou art very great! Thou art clothed with honor and majesty, who coverest thyself with light as with a garment, who hast stretched out the heavens like a tent, who hast laid the beams of thy chambers on the waters, who makest the clouds thy chariot, who ridest on the wings of the wind, who makest the winds thy messengers fire and flame thy ministers.

"And God made two great lights the greater light to rule the day . . ."   *Genesis 1:16*

"God divided the light from darkness . . .

. . . and the darkness He called night." *Genesis 1:16*

Thou didst set the earth on its foundations,
so that it should never be shaken. Thou didst cover
it with the deep as with a garment; the waters
stood above the mountains. At thy rebuke they fled; at the
sound of thy thunder they took to flight. The
mountains rose, the valleys sank down to the place which
thou didst appoint for them. Thou didst set a bound
which they should not pass, so that they
might not again cover the earth.

"And God said let the earth put forth vegetation . . ."

". . . plants yielding seed . . . and fruit trees
bearing fruit in which is their seed,
each according to its kind, upon the earth."

Genesis 1:11

"And God said let the waters bring forth swarms of living creatures." *Genesis 1:20*

Thou makest springs gush forth in the valleys;
they flow between the hills,
they drink to every beast of the field;

. . . the wild asses quench their thirst.
By them the birds of the air have their habitation;
they sing among the branches.

From thy lofty abode
thou waterest the mountains;
the earth is satisfied
with the fruit of thy work.

"...and God said let birds fly above the earth along heavens firmament." *Genesis 1:20, M.L.V.*

"... And God saw that it was good, and God blessed them, saying, be fruitful and multiply and fill the waters in the seas, and let birds multiply in the earth."

Genesis 1:21-22

"And God said:
  let the earth bring forth
  living creatures ..."
"... livestock ... reptiles ... wild beasts ..."
"... and it was so."

Genesis 1:24, M.L.V.

Thou dost cause the grass to grow for the cattle,
and plants for man to cultivate,
that he may bring forth food from the earth,
and wind to gladden the heart of man,
oil to make his face shine,
and bread to strengthen man's heart

The trees of the Lord are watered abundantly,
the cedars of Lebanon which he planted.

In them the birds build their nests;
the stork has her home in the fir trees.

The high mountains are for the wild goats;
the rocks are a refuge for the badgers.
Thou hast made the moon to mark the seasons;
the sun knows its time for setting.

Thou makest darkness, and it is night, when all the beasts
of the forest creep forth. The young lions
roar for their prey, seeking their food from God.
When the sun rises, they get them away and lie down
in their dens. Man goes forth to his work and to
his labor until the evening.

"Then God said let us make man in our image after
our likeness. So God created man in his own image . . ."
"And the Lord God formed the man from the dust of the
ground and breathed into his nostrils the breath of
life, and the man became a living soul."

Genesis 11:7

O Lord, how manifold are thy works!
In wisdom hast thou made them all;
the earth is full of thy creatures.
Yonder is the sea, great and wide,
which teems with things innumerable,
living things both small and great.
There go the ships, and Leviathan which
thou didst form to sport in it.

"God said . . . Fill the earth and subdue it; and have dominion over the fish of the sea the birds of the air and over every living thing that moves upon the earth." *Genesis 1:28*

These all look to thee, to give them their food in due season.
When thou givest to them, they gather it up;
when thou openest thy hand, they are filled with good things.
When thou hidest thy face, they are dismayed;
when thou takest away their breath, they die and return to their dust.
When thou sendest forth thy Spirit, they are
created; and thou renewest the face of the ground.

"Then the Lord God said, it is not good that the man should be alone."

Genesis 2:18

"I will make him a helper fit for him."

Genesis 2:18

"And God Blessed them and God said to them, be fruitful and multiply, and fill the earth . . ."

Genesis 1:28

"God saw everything that He made, and behold it was good." *Genesis 1:31*

May the glory of the Lord endure forever,
may the Lord rejoice in His works, who looks on the earth
and it trembles, who touches the mountains and
they smoke! I will sing to the Lord as long as I live:
I will sing praise to my God while I have being.
May my meditation be pleasing to Him, for
I rejoice in the Lord. Let sinners be consumed from
the earth, and let the wicked be no more! Bless the Lord,
O my soul! Praise the Lord!

The heavens are telling the glory of God;
and the firmament proclaims his handiwork; day to day
pours forth speech, and night to night declares
knowledge, there is no speech, nor are these words;
their voice goes out through all the earth, and
their words to the end of the world.

Psalm 19:1-4

"Ever since the creation of the world His invisible nature, namely, His eternal power and deity, has been clearly perceived in the things that have been made." *Romans 1:20*

"Have you not known? Have you not heard? Has it
not been told you from the beginning? Have you not
understood from the foundation of the earth? . . .
Lift up your eyes on high and see: who created these?"

Isaiah 40:21-26

"He covers the heavens with clouds, He prepares
rain for the earth, He makes grass grow upon the hills."

Psalm 147:8